Fun with Grammar

SENTENCES AND PARAGRAPHS

Casey is going swimming.

Emily and Amy went to the store.

Samantha Green

Enslow Publishing
101 W. 23rd Street
Suite 240
New York, NY 10011
USA
enslow.com

Words to Know

advice Guidance about what you should do.

capital The larger form of a letter that starts a sentence.

common Normal or regular.

discuss To talk or write about something.

object The thing the verb is talking about in a sentence.

subject The person or thing that is being talked about in a sentence.

topic sentence The sentence that communicates the main idea of a paragraph.

Contents

“John is reading.”
This is a sentence.

What Is a Sentence?

A sentence is a group of words put together. Every sentence is about one idea. Sentences can be long or short, but they all need a noun and a verb.

Fast Fact

We speak and write in sentences.

We use punctuation marks to separate different ideas into different sentences.

What Is in a Sentence?

Sentences start with a **capital** letter and end with a punctuation mark. Periods, exclamation points, and question marks can all end sentences.

Plays is another verb.
"The dog plays outside."

Sentence Order

Sentences have a specific order: **subject**, verb, **object**. The subject is whom or what the sentence is about. The object is what the verb is talking about. "The dog loves dirt." The word *dog* is the subject, and *dirt* is the object.

Fast Fact

Verbs are action words. Above, *loves* is the verb!

Statements usually end with a period.

Statements

Sentences that share information or ideas are called statements. They are the most **common** type of sentence.

Questions teach us things. We might ask, "What do you want for your birthday?"

Questions

Questions are sentences that ask for information. They end with a question mark. The word order in a question is different from the order in a statement.

Fast Fact

"When is the party?" The verb *is* comes before the subject *party*.

The subject in a command sentence is always the same, even though you don't see it: You!

Commands

Sometimes, sentences tell listeners and readers what to do. Command sentences can give us **advice** or directions.

"Pass the chocolate."

"Stop running!"

Fast Fact

These sentences do not have subjects because it is understood that the listener or reader is the subject.

"I am happy!" shows more excitement than "I am happy."

Exclamations

Sentences that use a lot of emotion are exclamations! They usually end with an exclamation point. They can show happy, sad, or angry emotions.

Paragraphs help make up reports and papers.

What Is a Paragraph?

A paragraph is a group of sentences that focus on a single idea. Paragraphs can tell a story or state what someone thinks.

Fast Fact

Paragraphs can be as short as one sentence!

Your teacher might have rules about the number of sentences in a paragraph.

Putting a Paragraph Together

A paragraph has one main idea that is **discussed** through multiple sentences. It starts with a **topic sentence**. Next come sentences that prove the topic sentence or give examples.

Fast Fact

New paragraphs always start on the next line.

We form our thoughts into sentences so that we're able to talk with other people.

Powerful Sentences and Paragraphs

Sentences put words together to make sure our ideas are understood. Then, we can create paragraphs to build on our sentences and put our thoughts into writing.

Learn More

Books

Mercury, Dria L. *Sight Words and Short Sentences.* New York, NY: CreateSpace Independent Publishing Platform, 2015.

Murray, Kara. *Simple and Compound Sentences.* New York, NY: PowerKids Press, 2014.

Websites

Cookie.com: Simple Sentences
http://www.cookie.com/kids/games/simple-sentences.html
Learn to put together simple sentences with games and activities.

Turtle Diary: Sentence Structure Games
https://www.turtlediary.com/games/sentences.html
Play fun games and learn the right punctuation to use for different sentences.

Index

Published in 2020 by Enslow Publishing, LLC.
101 W. 23rd Street, Suite 240, New York, NY 10011

Library of Congress Cataloging-in-Publication Data

Names: Green, Samantha, author.
Title: Sentences and paragraphs / Samantha Green.
Description: New York : Enslow, 2020. | Series: Fun with grammar | Audience:
Grades: 1–4. | Includes bibliographical references and index.Identifiers: LCCN 2019013431 | ISBN 9781978512757 (library bound) | ISBN 9781978512733 (pbk.) | ISBN 9781978512740 (6 pack) Subjects: LCSH: English language—Sentences—Juvenile literature. | English language—Paragraphs—Juvenile literature. | English language—Grammar—Juvenile literature. | Composition (Language arts)—Juvenile literature.
Classification: LCC PE1441 .G73 2020 | DDC 428.2—dc23

LC record available at https://lccn.loc.gov/2019013431

Printed in the United States of America

Photo Credits: Cover, p. 1 Rawpixel.com/Shutterstock.com; cover, p. 1 (pencil) OrangeVector/Shutterstock.com; p. 4 Africa Studio/Shutterstock.com; p. 6 Yayayoyo/Shutterstock.com; p. 8 Ekaterina Karetkina/Shutterstock.com; p. 10 Gelpi/Shutterstock.com; p. 12 Prostock-studio/Shutterstock.com; p. 14 AzmanJaka/iStock/Getty Images; p. 16 Mandy Godbehear/Shutterstock.com; p. 18 Romiana Lee/Shutterstock.com; p. 20 wavebreakmedia/Shutterstock.com; p. 22 asiseeit/E+/Getty Images; interior pages (notebook) Fascinadora/Shutterstock.com; interior pages (pencil) spacezerocom/Shutterstock.com.